T0381323

The "Hairy" Adventures of Benjamin P. Hartford

Susan Parton Wright

Illustrator: Niki Price

AuthorHouse™
1663 Liberty Drive
Bloomington, IN 47403
www.authorhouse.com
Phone: 1 (833) 262-8899

Because of the dynamic nature of the Internet, any web addresses or links contained in this book may have changed
since publication and may no longer be valid. The views expressed in this work are solely those of the author and do not
necessarily reflect the views of the publisher, and the publisher hereby disclaims any responsibility for them.

Any people depicted in stock imagery provided by Getty Images are models,
and such images are being used for illustrative purposes only.
Certain stock imagery © Getty Images.

This book is printed on acid-free paper.

ISBN: 978-1-4389-2455-7 (sc)

Print information available on the last page.

Published by AuthorHouse 09/22/2020

authorHOUSE®

Chapter 1

"Good morning, Benji," Benjamin P. Hartford said to himself as he opened his eyes to begin what was to become a most interesting day. Benji raced across the hallway and into the bathroom. He could hear his mother and father downstairs. His mother cooked breakfast while his father talked on and on about his plans for the day. Benji turned on the bathroom light and scrunched his eyes tightly, trying to block out the blinding light. He dreaded opening them because he knew his hair would be a mess, as usual. His hair was so curly that no one had successfully gotten a comb through it since the first hair had appeared eight years ago. He also hated the color of his hair. It was dirty blond and looked like the water after you washed the dishes.

"Benjamin Porter Hartford, have you combed your hair today?" his mother would ask.

"Mary, you really must do something about the boy's hair," his father would say.

"Benji has a rat's nest on his head," his sister, Marcy, *always* said.

When Benji opened his eyes, he nearly fainted. The sight was unbelievable— sitting on top of his head was a family, a whole family, of mice. Benjamin moved closer to the mirror and blinked his eyes several times, but they were still there. It was not his imagination playing tricks on him. When Benji looked closer, he could see that the mice were staring back at him.

"Hey," called the largest of the mice. "How are you this fine morning?"

Benji did not know what to say; he had never had a mouse speak to him before.

"N-n-nothing," Benji stuttered.

"Well, I am Royster T. Mouse, and these here are my brothers, Harold and Ludwig. We really think we are going to enjoy staying here."

"What are you doing here?" Benji asked.

"Well, you see," said Ludwig, "we've been looking for a place to stay since the weather is turning cold."

"And," began Harold, "we heard someone say that you had a rat's nest on your head, so we thought—"

Royster piped in, "We would check it out."

Benjamin stood there mouth hanging open. What could he do? He couldn't let anyone see him. Suddenly there was a knock at the door.

"Hurry up, booger head," screamed Marcy.

Marcy, Benjamin panicked, *she must* not *find out*.

Quickly he grabbed a towel and threw it over his head. Benji opened the door and ran across the hall to his room.

"It's about time," Marcy yelled as she slammed the bathroom door.

Benji quickly shut his door and flung the towel onto the floor.

"Whew," Ludwig yelled, "what did you do that for?"

"You guys cannot stay here," Benji yelled. "I'll be laughed out of town."

He paced the floor trying to decide what to do.

"Benjamin," his mother called from the kitchen, "you and Marcy need to get down here. Breakfast is ready, and church is in forty-five minutes."

Church, Benjamin thought, *I can't go, not today*.

He knew his mom would never allow him to miss church. He would have to think of some way to hide the mice; after all, they didn't have anywhere else to go. Benjamin dressed quickly and picked up his Sunday hat. The hat had belonged to Benji's grandfather. Benji used to wear it to church, but that was when he was four years old. Everyone had thought it was cute then, but now that he was eight and a half, what would they think? As he came out of his bedroom, Marcy was going down the stairs. Benji ducked back inside to give her time to get out of his way. Then he walked downstairs quietly and into the kitchen, hoping not to be noticed.

"Come on, Benjamin; the pancakes are getting cold," his mom called.

"You want milk or juice?" his father asked.

"Milk. Milk. Milk," called the three mice from underneath Benji's hat.

Benji coughed loudly to try to block out the voices.

"Okay, okay," his father said. "Once is enough, son; I'm getting it."

His father looked annoyed. "Benjamin, why do you have that hat on inside the house? Besides, you haven't worn that hat in years."

"Well, Dad," Benji chose his words carefully. "I was thinking this morning about how distinguished Grandpa Parker was and--"

"You don't look 'stinguished," Marcy yelled.

"Marcy, that is quite enough," her mother scolded.

"Tee-hee-hee." Harold, the youngest mouse, was snickering from underneath the hat. Again, Benji coughed, trying to cover up the noise. Luckily, Benji's mother noticed the time and forgot all about the hat.

"Hurry, hurry. It's almost time to go!" said Mrs. Hartford as she scurried around the kitchen.

Benjamin got up and tucked a pancake into his pocket.

"Benjamin, where are you going?" Marcy called as he headed upstairs. "Mama said to go to the car."

"I have to brush my teeth," Benji called and ran upstairs.

Benji ran into the bathroom. He took the hat off, only to find the three mice playing a game of charades.

"Three words. First word," Harold yelled, "sounds like ..."

Suddenly the mice noticed that Benji had removed the hat.

"Hey, yo, Ben," Royster called, "what say ya lose the hat. I mean it's hard to play charades when you can barely see."

"Yeah," Harold added, "Ludwig ain't too 'bright' as it is."

"HA, HA, HA!" the three mice cracked up.

"Hey," Ludwig said, "what did you say?"

Royster and Harold howled with laughter at Ludwig's expense.

"Here," Benjamin said, breaking the pancake into three parts. "Eat this, and please be quiet in church."

Benji threw the hat over his head and ran downstairs without even brushing his teeth.

Sunday school was no problem because Mr. Rudolf ran a tight ship. Mr. Rudolf was the very reason it was called Sunday *school.*

"No talking," said Mr. Rudolf.

"No whispering," said Mr. Rudolf.

"No breathing!" was what Benji expected to hear from him next.

However, today, Benjamin was thankful for Mr. Rudolf because his strictness would keep Billy Brenkle from being able to tease him about the hat. Mr. Hartford had explained the hat to Mr. Rudolf, who gladly let the hat stay on the head of the "thoughtful young man." Sunday school ended without incident, and Benji went directly to the sanctuary so as to avoid the ragging of one Billy Brenkle.

The mice had been quiet during Sunday school. Apparently they, too, feared the wrath of Mr. Rudolf. The mice were quiet during the hymns—or at least Benjamin guessed they were. But then again, who could hear over the soprano voice of Mrs. Ruby McFarland? However, halfway through Reverend Tollison's sermon--

"Zzzzzzzz."

Uh-oh, Benji thought. *Please, no!*

Benji was hoping he wasn't hearing what he thought he was hearing.

"Zzzzzzzz!" There it was again.

Suddenly, everyone began to look around to find the snorer. Benjamin squirmed in his seat and scuffled his feet as he tried to mask the noise.

"Zzzzzzzz"

The snore was getting louder and louder, and it was only a matter of time before he was discovered as the boy with a rodent motel on his head.

I should cough, Benji thought, and he started coughing quietly and got louder and louder. His mother shot him an evil look, to which Benji replied with a *who-me?* look. He waited a few minutes and began coughing again. Mrs. Hartford rummaged through her purse and found a peppermint that had come unwrapped and probably had been at the bottom of her purse since 1983. She shoved the mint toward Benji; he dared not eat it.

"Zzzzzzzzzzzzzzz"

The snoring was getting so loud that wives began elbowing their husbands just in case they were sleeping with their eyes open.

"Cough, cough," Benjamin continued, until his mother whispered—she really yelled but did so in a whisper—"Go get some water."

Benji got up and nearly ran out the back door. He ran into the bathroom and into a stall and removed his hat quickly.

He had only had the hat off a few seconds when Ludwig yelled, "Turn off those lights."

"I am trying to sleep here," Harold added.

But Royster continued to snore.

"You guys have got to stop making so much noise," Benji pleaded.

"Hey, hey," Royster cried. "What's all the racket? And where's the man that put us to sleep? He tells the best bedtime stories."

"That was Reverend Tollison and it was not a bedtime story," Benji explained.

"Well, he sure put us to sleep," Harold laughed.

"Benji!" a voice called out.

Dad, Benji panicked. What could he do?

He threw the hat back onto his head.

"Hey, hey!" called the mice as the lights suddenly went out.

"Just a second, Dad. We'll … I'll be right out," Benjamin called through the stall door.

Benji took a second to gather his thoughts and walked out to meet his father.

"Son, are you okay?" his dad asked.

"Sure, Dad, just a nasty coughing spell. I'm okay now," Benji, answered.

"Hey, Ben," Royster called out. "Yo, Ben, my man!"

Benji reacted with yet another coughing spell.

"What was that?" asked his dad, completely puzzled.

"Benny, we need some light in here," yelled Ludwig.

With that, Mr. Hartford pulled the hat from his son's head and got the surprise of his life.

"Wh-wh-what the ..." Mr. Hartford was dumbfounded.

"Hold on, Dad. I can explain," Benji said.

Suddenly, Mr. Banks, the choir director, entered the restroom, and Mr. Hartford threw the hat onto his son's head.

"Come on, son. Let's get you home," he said to Benji.

"The boy sick?" asked Mr. Banks.

"No, just a nasty cough," answered Mr. Hartford as he escorted Benjamin to the car.

In a few minutes, his mother and Marcy arrived.

"Are you okay, honey?" Mrs. Hartford asked.

"He's fine," Mr. Hartford said.

"Did you puke?" his little sister asked.

Everyone looked at Marcy with disgust.

"No!" they all yelled at once.

"We're trying to sleep in here," came a voice from underneath Benji's hat.

Mrs. Hartford and Marcy looked directly at Benji. Realizing it could not have been him, they looked confused.

"Mary, hon, I have something to tell you," said Mr. Hartford slowly.

"What is it, Ben?" Mrs. Hartford said nervously.

"Benjamin, please remove your hat, and, Marcy, no matter what, you keep quiet," he said.

Slowly, Benji pulled the hat from his head. Slowly, he placed the hat in the seat between him and his sister.

"Now, Mary, honey, turn around and try to stay calm," said Mr. Hartford as he stared in the rearview mirror.

Benji's mother turned around and let out a gasp that contained a partial scream.

"Ben, exactly what is going on here?" Mrs. Hartford asked.

Benji looked over at his sister who was sitting with her mouth hanging open staring directly at her brother's head.

"She's speechless," Benji said. "Oh well, there is a first time for everything."

The rest of the way home Mr. Hartford and Benji explained the situation to Mrs. Hartford and Marcy, who still had not shut her mouth. In fact, she had begun to drool disgustingly. Ludwig, Harold, and Royster had been quiet ever since the hat had been pulled and they had heard the horrible gasp from Mrs. Hartford. In fact, all three of them stood there as if they were imitating Marcy.

When they arrived home, Mrs. Hartford had to shake Marcy several times to get her attention. The family and the rats went inside to decide what they would do. Mr. Hartford mapped out a plan. First, they would make a home for the three mice in one of Benji's drawers—preferably the sock drawer. Second, Benji's hair would have to be cut, maybe even shaved, to prevent rodents from taking up residence there in future. Finally, Marcy *must* stop referring to anyone's hair as a rat's nest. After all, mice obviously take such descriptions very seriously.

Royster had listened to the plan intently, and he waited to speak until he was sure Mr. H had finished.

"Excuse me, ma'am," Royster said, "but my brothers and I highly object to the first part of the plan."

"Yeah," added Harold, "we ain't gonna live in no smelly sock drawer."

"Besides," piped up Ludwig, "it will be dark, and Roy always says I ain't too bright as it is."

"Mom," Benji said, "I don't really want to have my head shaved, please."

"Now, now," Mrs. Hartford began, "your dad's plan may have a few kinks in it, but it's a start."

"Well, I agree with my part, Mama," said Marcy.

Everyone stared in disbelief as she continued. "I'm finished making fun of people, even Benji. After this—"

Everyone clapped for Marcy.

"At least some good has come of this," said Mr. Hartford, hugging Marcy.

They discussed their plans as they ate dinner. Mr. Hartford made a place for the mice at Marcy's dollhouse dining table. The mice hungrily dined on mac 'n' cheese and cheesecake. During dessert, Marcy let out a yell that caused everyone to jump.

"I've got it. I've got it," she screamed.

"What is it, honey?" Mrs. Hartford asked.

"My dollhouse, Mommy—the mice can live in my dollhouse. I mean it has lights that really work and everything," said Marcy.

The mice stopped eating to listen; this sounded good to them—their own home. They decided to voice their opinion.

"Mr. and Mrs. Hartford," Royster spoke up. "If I may be so bold as to give our opinion on the subject."

"Go right ahead," Mrs. Hartford said, "please."

"Well, my brothers and I love the idea of our own home complete with lights. But I do have to ask, how many bedrooms are in this lovely home?" he inquired.

"It has three," Marcy said, "and two bathrooms, but they don't really work," she added.

"Did you hear that, Roy?" Ludwig cried. "We'll each have our own room."

"Shhh!" shushed Royster.

He motioned for his brothers to sit down and let the family make a decision.

"What do you think, son?" asked Mr. Hartford. "Do you like the idea?"

Benji had thought the mice would stay with him, but he sure didn't want a dollhouse in his room.

"Royster, are you three willing to live in Marcy's room?" Benji asked.

"Sure!" Royster said as the other two sat nodding their heads frantically.

"I promise I'll be good," Marcy said.

"It's settled then," Mrs. Hartford said. "Right after dinner, we'll get things ready."

Mrs. Hartford got busy sewing curtains for each of the rooms. Luckily, she had scraps of cloth from the last costume she had made Benji for Halloween. She made black curtains for Harold, who had trouble sleeping when there was too much light. She made white curtains for Ludwig, since he was "not too bright" and, as Harold put it, "needed as much light as possible." She made green curtains for Royster because, well because that was the only other color she had. After completing the curtains, she set about trying to find old towels and wash cloths from which to make sheets and blankets. The entire process took about an hour and a half. By that time, Mr. Hartford had the dollhouse set up in Marcy's room. Then Marcy and the mice arranged the furniture. Ludwig chose the upstairs bedroom, leaving the two downstairs for his brothers, which suited Royster because he could see Marcy's television perfectly from his bedroom window.

Chapter 2

The mice lived a quiet, uneventful life with the Hartford's—well, the first few months were uneventful. Then came October eighth. What happened on October eighth can only be described as … well, to quote Royster, "a disaster, a total disaster," and to quote Marcy, "the biggest *oops* ever," and to quote Mrs. Hartford, "Oh my gosh; oh my gracious goodness."Let's first examine the events that led up to the "oops". Royster, Ludwig, and Harold had made the dollhouse their home. Why, they even had a teeny mailbox, in which Postmaster Marcy delivered their mail daily. Ludwig especially loved it when their "Cheese of the Month" would arrive; that usually happened on the third Thursday. It would be Ludwig's turn to cook on that particular day. He would make soufflés, bread puddings, and other such goodies with the cheese. He even made cheese popsicles once, but no one would eat them.

The rooms were well furnished, and the water ran hot and cold throughout, thanks to Mr. Hartford's wonderful plumbing skills. Harold had fallen in love with taking bubble baths. He would run a bath, pour in the sweet-smelling bubbles, pour himself a warm mug of milk, and listen to Chee Zee's greatest hits. He usually stayed in the tub until his skin was like a prune. This made Ludwig laugh; he always said that Harold looked just like their great-grandma, Thora Dean, with his wrinkly fingers and toes. One night, she packed up everything she owned and moved to do "research." The boys had heard that she had all she wanted to eat and run around on a wheel all day. They'd always imagined having that kind of life, and now they were living even better than was Grandma Thora.

The mice spent their days lying around watching television and playing games. Their favorite show was *The Price is Right*. The minute Harold and Ludwig heard the intro music, they were glued to the TV. Ludwig rather fancied cooking shows. "Bam" had become his new catch phrase, thanks to his favorite chef. This, however, caused some problems because, ever since the July Fourth fireworks celebration, his brothers would hit the floor whenever Royster would let out the dreaded "bam."

When Benji and Marcy were out of school, the mice would beg to play with them. Marcy loved to play dress up with them, but Ludwig was the only one who could tolerate this. In fact, he actually liked it. He really liked it when they played makeover, but the powder she used on his face made him sneeze something fierce. Benji would set up his army men so Harold and Royster could go around "inspecting the troops." Oh how the mice loved weekends and holidays.

On October First, Mrs. Hartford's mother, Mary Ellen Parker, came to visit. Grandma Parker, as the kids referred to her, lived about sixty miles away and came up for weekends and holidays. The kids loved it when their grandma came to visit because she always brought presents, and she baked for them. Benji had already warned the mice about Grandma Parker's visit. He'd asked them to lay low until she left. Mr. Hartford had moved the dollhouse into Benji's closet until the visitor was gone.

"Intruder" is the way Harold referred to Mrs. Parker.

On October Second, Grandma decided that she would love to help her daughter with the garage sale she had been planning for months and months. It had been, in fact, so long in the planning stages that it had started as a good way to get rid of the baby things. After all, Marcy, her youngest, was five years old now. Grandma was up early clearing out closets. She had a huge box in the middle of the living room. The box contained rattles, crib toys, a potty chair, stuffed toys, and other such things.

Marcy was whining to her mother. "Mommy, I loved that potty … not my binky." On and on Marcy went.

This made Benji laugh and wonder how a five-year-old could become so attached to things. It never entered Benji's mind that Grandma Parker had not rifled through his room yet. At 11:00 a.m., Matt and George called and invited Benji to come over and play kickball with them. He was so glad it wasn't raining today, as it had been for the past few days.

"Mom," Benji yelled, "going to Matt's."

His grandma grabbed him on the way out the door.

"Benny, hon." OOOHHHH, how he hated it when she called him Benny. "Is your room clean? Grandma's going to get things for the garage sale."

"Yeah, Grandma. I made my bed and put away my toys," he said as he ran out the door.

Then he remembered something very important, so he ran back into the house. He yelled at Grandma as she climbed the stairs, "Grandma, don't sell my Legos. I still play with them."

Mary Ellen entered Benji's room "at her own risk," which is what the sign on the door said. She was surprised at how neat it was. The bed had been made properly, and all the toys were in their proper place. She was very impressed.

Then suddenly they saw the closet door open. Royster ran and looked out the window.

"Oh no; it's Ben's grandma."

"Hey!" yelled Ludwig.

Royster threw his finger up to his lips—"Shhhh!"and pointed to the closet door.

Each mouse went to his room and tried to be as quiet as … well, a mouse.

Grandma picked up rubber baseballs, jack sets, stuffed toys—you name it, she picked it up. Then suddenly, she spied the dollhouse. She walked over and peeked inside.

Hmmmmm, this must be Marcy's, and she surely doesn't play with it if it's stuck back in Benji's closet, she thought.

She made a mental note to get it tomorrow morning.

Benji and Marcy looked through the garage sale items when dinner was over. There was not even one thing that they felt that they could not let go of, except maybe Marcy's baby blue elephant. The funny thing was that she never played with the elephant, but now she just could not seem to part with it.

"Well, sleep with it tonight, Marcy," her mom said, "and if you are still attached to it in the morning, then you may keep it."

Fair 'nuf, thought Marcy.

"I'm going to my room for awhile," Benji winked to his mom.

She placed some scraps of food into his hand. "Sure, Benji," said his mom. "Why don't you spend some time reading alone?"

"Good idea, Mom; can always bring my reading grade up."

Uuuummmmm," slurped Ludwig, "noodles with Alfredo sauce, my favorite."

"It's all your favorite, Lud," said Royster, as he nibbled on a couple of ears of baby corn.

"The salad is scrumptious," chimed in Harold. "My compliments to the chef."

The mice ate and ate until they fell back in pain. They loved Mrs. Hartford's cooking. After they ate, Benji read them a bedtime story. He read the one about the three blind mice. This story always made them realize just how truly lucky they were. "Imagine," Ludwig always said, "someone cutting off our tails with a carving knife."

Then Harold would start howling with laughter and add, "I just couldn't *see* it."

"HA HA HA!" he would roar with laughter, even when he was the only one laughing.

Ludwig and Harold slept like babies that night, but poor Royster just couldn't get to sleep. Benji had left the closet door cracked so that they could just see a hint of light from his nightlight. After tossing and turning for a while, Royster got up, making his way toward Benji's bed. He climbed over sneakers, around balls and bats, and through the slinky. Finally, he made it to the bed. He grabbed hold of the covers and heaved himself upward.

"Psst, yo, Ben!" Royster whispered. "Ben, my man, are you sleeping?"

Benji opened his eyes and immediately recognized Royster's voice. Yawning, he asked, "What's up, Roy?"

"Well I don't quite know," said the mouse. "I just couldn't sleep."

Benji tried to reassure him, to let him know that everything was going to be okay. They talked for a long time about music, sports, even the weather, until Royster was ready for bed. Benji carried him back to his home in the closet. He heard Ludwig snoring and Harold talking in his sleep, oh how he

wished he could understand him. If only he didn't mumble when he talked in his sleep.

"Goodnight, Royster," said Benji. "I will be watching over you all as usual."

"I know," said Royster as he went inside and shut the door.

Chapter 3

Morning came a little too quickly for Mary Ellen. She had been up late watching infomercials. She yawned and yawned when her clock alarmed 5:30 that morning. She wanted to get the garage sale items priced. She headed downstairs to start her coffee. As it brewed, she made herself some toast. Suddenly out of the corner of her eye, she thought she saw a mouse.

"Yikes," she screamed, softly of course, as to not wake the family.

Then she scurried around trying to locate the rodent.

Whew, close call, thought Harold. *Why must cheese tempt me so much*?

He had been watching an infomercial about a toaster oven when they made a grilled cheese sandwich and, viola, the next thing he remembered he was standing in front of the fridge trying to reach the cheese. When Harold heard the scream, he thought he saw his short little life pass before his eyes, but he didn't have time for a matinee; he had to run. He ran across the floor only to have a broom chasing him. Just before the broom caught him, he dashed underneath the refrigerator. He was afraid that this would be his end; however, he saw feet begin to disappear from sight.

Harold eased his head out from under the appliance. The coast was clear, so he ran across the kitchen floor and up the stairs. Once he stopped and hid in the sneaker Marcy had left on the top step because he swore he heard Grandma's fluffy slippers closing in on him. Just as the smell of the sneaker was getting to him, he peeked out of the shoe and made his way back to the closet, back to the safety of his house.

Ludwig awoke suddenly, to what sounded like the front door banging shut. He pulled himself out of bed and went to the living room to see what the racket was all about. There was Harold standing against the front door looking like he had seen a ghost.

"Harold, what were you doing out there at night?" Ludwig asked.

"I don't remember," Harold gasped, "but I am not going out there again until *she* leaves."

Ludwig knew that by *she* Harold meant Benji's grandma; that woman had been trouble for them since the first day she arrived. There had not been one minute when the mice had felt at ease, even in their own home. They knew that, if she had even an inkling that they were in the house, it would be the end for them.

"Harold," Ludwig whispered, "just go back to bed, buddy; you'll feel better in the morning."

Harold went to bed, just happy to still be in one piece.

The days afterward passed quickly, and Saturday morning was the garage sale. Benji's mom and grandma were up bright and early. Marcy had already yelled downstairs to tell them to "hold down the racket," and Mr. Hartford had already left to go to play golf, for he wanted nothing to do with this nonsense. Benji pulled the covers over his head and fell fast asleep, dreaming he was 007, and the mice were his sidekicks. They were chasing villains. Mary Ellen entered Benji's closet. She removed the dollhouse that she'd spied days before.

Ludwig, Harold, and Royster snored away inside, not knowing that they were being relocated. When Mrs. Parker sat the dollhouse out onto the carport, the mice couldn't tell, thanks to the insulation Mr. Hartford had placed around the doors and windows when he had renovated.

Mrs. Pettigrew was the first customer. Mrs. Pettigrew lived just down the street and was the mother of "little" Leeann Pettigrew. Leeann was the "biggest brat on the planet," according to Marcy. Leann and Marcy had been in the same kindergarten class, and they had never gotten along. Benji always thought it was just because they both were the "biggest brat on the planet," and neither could stand the competition.

Mrs. Pettigrew talked with Mary Ellen for a while. They talked about the weather, the price of gasoline, the price of food—you name it, they talked about it. Mrs. Pettigrew mentioned that she was looking for something to buy Leeann for being so brave at the doctor's office yesterday.

"Well, just look around," Mary Ellen said. "You're sure to find something."

Royster awoke with a start; he had not slept this late on a Saturday morning in awhile. He sat up in the bed and stretched. He thought he heard voices, but they seemed muffled.

"Ben must be watching TV," he thought.

He climbed out of bed. On his way to the bathroom, he stopped by the window and peeked out.

Oh my, he thought. *Where are we?*

Suddenly, he recognized the scenery—well not exactly, but he knew they were *not* in the closet. Royster made his way to Harold's room

"Harold," he whispered.

"Sure I would love some more," Harold said, obviously talking in his sleep.

Royster shook him awake and threw his hand over his mouth. "Shhhh, Harold; Harold, listen," Royster explained. "We've got trouble. You go get Ludwig; we have to get out of here."

"But, but," Harold protested. After all, he had been dreaming of that Italian girl on that food show, and she had been serving him the most delicious cheese and wine.

Reluctantly, he crept down the hallway with his brother. All of a sudden, they heard voices.

"Leeann would love this," Mrs. Pettigrew said.

As she said this, she opened the front door of the dollhouse.

Royster and Harold each dove into the hall closet.

"Th-th-that's Benji's grandma," whispered Harold. "But who is Leeann?"

"I don't know," said Royster, "but we need to get Ludwig and get out of here."

The front door shut, but the voices continued.

"That is lovely," said Mrs. Pettigrew. "What are you asking for it?"

"Well," said Mary Ellen, "Marcy hasn't played with it for a while now, so maybe ten dollars."

"Hmmmmm, let me look around a little," Mrs. Pettigrew said shrewdly, thinking that she could wait Mary Ellen out and get a better price. After all, was that not the game played out at all garage sales? She looked through everything—the balls, the puzzles, the games, everything—but she simply could not take her eyes off the dollhouse.

Royster and Harold opened the front door a tiny bit, just enough to peek out. The coast looked clear.

"Harold, you stay right here. I'm going to try to make it to Ludwig's room to get him," Royster explained.

"You had better get out of here. If we don't make it," Royster added, tearing up, "it's been great."

"Don't make it. Don't make it!" yelled Harold. "What do you mean don't make it?"

But Royster was already gone.

"Mary Ellen," said Mrs. Pettigrew. "I'll take the dollhouse. Leeann is sure to love it."

"Excellent choice," said Mrs. Parker. "That will be $9.99."

That is, briefly, how the big *oops* came about.

Harold had his nose stuck out the kitchen window hoping to hop out and make it to the "big house." Suddenly, the house lurched, and the ground got farther and farther away. Harold dropped back into the sink, thinking he would never see his brothers again.

Ludwig, he thought, *I must find him.*

Jumping down, he scurried up the steps and ran smack into Ludwig as he ran down.

"Harold, Royster, the house is moving!" Ludwig shouted.

"I know, I know, and Benji's grandma has something to do with it. Didn't Royster find you."

The brothers ran into the living room closet to hide, hoping, Royster had somehow managed to escape.

Meanwhile, Royster was running to the house knowing his brothers only help was Benji himself.

"Meow!"

The sound stopped Royster dead in his tracks.

"*Oh no!*" he thought, almost afraid to raise his head.

Princess, the neighbor's cat, was standing to his right, and without looking Roy knew she was talking to him.

Play dead, he thought.

After all, he had seen this on those animal shows; it worked with bears, and everyone knew that cats were not nearly as bright as bears. Immediately, Royster fell down onto the grass, arms outstretched, tongue wagging. Princess came closer, sniffing Royster's fur.

"Oh my gosh, Mom," said a tiny voice.

Royster opened one eye and noticed a smaller version of Princess standing beside her.

"Have we kilt him, Mama?" she said. "I sure hope not. After all, I wanted to play with him," she continued.

Princess started to paw him, pushing and shoving. Then she started rubbing his side. Royster tried hard not to laugh, but this was, after all, his "tickle spot," as his brothers always called it. They had spent days upon days tickling him, often sending him into hysterics. Royster tried hard, very hard, not to laugh, but whom was he kidding. He burst into laughter. Princess crouched, growling loudly.

"Missy," Princess said to the smaller version of her, "do this."

Missy crouched down falling face first into Royster's fur.

"Missy, Missy," an exasperated Princess said, "just go back home. We'll try again tomorrow."

The cats ran back to the neighbor's house, and Royster breathed a huge sigh of relief. He did not, however, have time to sit here thinking of what could have been; he had to get into that house and find Benji.

The door to the house was shut tight.

Now what? thought Royster.

He walked around the house looking up at every window; of course, they were all shut and locked. Then he remembered that Harold had climbed through the vent one night when he was having one of his nightmares. Royster ran to the back of the house, trying to judge which was the window to Marcy's room because he remembered that he'd been sitting in the window wishing on a star when he'd seen Harold climb out of the vent.

Just then, he spied the hole. He climbed over the azalea, over the ivy, and onto the vent. Poking his head through, he realized he should have been watching his waistline. He sucked in his gut, pulled and tugged, and almost made it all the way inside.

"Meow."

He scrambled

"Meooowww!"

Princess again, he thought.

"Mousey, where are you?" Princess sang.

"Come on back and play," she begged.

One more push, and he would be inside. Royster held his breath, and *boom*, he fell inside into the laundry basket.

Peeewwwww! thought Royster. *Wouldn't ya know it—stinky socks.*

However, right now he was thankful for the stinky socks. After all, he couldn't very well help his brothers with a broken hip, now could he? Royster climbed up the side of the basket, dropping onto the floor of the laundry room.

"Take a right, down the hall, up the stairs, first room on the left," Royster mumbled the directions to Benji's room.

Now he had to hope and pray that the door was open. Royster ran out the door and took a right; the coast was clear, so off he went. The hallway may as well have been an obstacle course. First up were Marcy's bunny slippers; Royster remembered that those fuzzy, pink slippers had caused him to nearly have a heart attack when he'd come upon them in the dark one night. He dodged the slippers and ran headfirst into a gigantic—at least to a tiny rodent—red, round thing. Marcy called this thing a kickball, and as long as he had lived here, he had never seen her play with it. He'd started around the ball when it began rolling toward him.

Yikes, thought Royster, and he ran full throttle down the hall. Just as the ball hit his heel, he dove up the stairs.

"Whew!" said Royster falling back against the next step. Each step was a chore, but the mouse took each one as quickly as possible, knowing the importance of his mission. As he conquered the last step, he heard the front door open.

"Marcy, Benji," said a voice.

Oh no. It can't be, he thought, *not her, not now.*

Royster jumped underneath the table just to his left in the upstairs hallway.

"Are you kids up yet?" Grandma Parker said a she climbed the stairs. "Yoo-hoo, children!"

Oh, how Royster would love to run across her sparkling white Keds just to listen to her scream, but right now he must focus, he *had* to save his brothers.

"Benny, hon, get up, sweetie," Grandma Parker sang, pushing the door open and turning to go back down the stairs.

"What is this?" she asked herself aloud as she bent down.

Royster held his breath and tried to melt into the leg of the table. Mrs. Parker's hand reached underneath the table, just barely missing Royster. Just then, she grabbed the yellow sock.

How did she see that? thought Royster. Why, he hadn't even seen it. Once she had retrieved the sock, she was off again to do who knows what.

Benji was yawning and stretching, Royster could hear him. The mouse peeked out from under the table then ran full speed into the boy's room. Thankfully, Benji was such a fitful sleeper—Royster was able to use the blanket that had fallen to the floor as a means to get to Benji. He felt like that guy—what was his name?—Indiana Jones. He had seen Indiana when the family had a retro-movie night.

As he reached the top, he yelled, "Yo, Ben! Yo, Ben!"

Benji turned his head, only to have a cute little mouse staring him in the face.

"Roy, why are you out of the closet?

Immediately Royster cut him off. "Hold it, Ben. First, I was *outside*, and that grandma of yours is solely responsible for that fact." He had to stop and take a breath.

"Thanks to her, my brothers are now in the hands of some woman with curlers in her hair."

As soon as Benji heard this, he was out of bed, mouse in hand.

"What?" he yelled.

"Okay, it's a long story, Ben, and I can give you the details later, but listen," he said. "Your grandma sold our house to some lady, and my brothers are still inside."

Royster looked up at Benji, hoping his friend would have a plan to get his brothers back; they were sometimes pains, but he loved them after all. Benji sat on the edge of the bed thinking.

"Well, I could … Well we will …"

Royster listened intently, but Benji never finished a sentence.

"You could what?" yelled the mouse. "We will what?"

Benji opened his mouth, for what Royster thought was to give him hope, but Benji yelled, "Marcy, Marcy, get in here—*now*, please."

When Marcy didn't show up, Benji and Royster headed for her room.

Royster thought, *This used to be* our *room too.*

"Sis, get up. We need your help," Benji yelled.

Marcy rolled over and pulled the covers tight over her head.

"Get *out*!" she yelled. *"now!"*

Benji grabbed the covers and yanked them off his sister.

"Eeewwwww," yelled the boy and the mouse in unison.

Marcy's gown was bunched up, and they could see Marcy's underwear.

"We see London. We see France. We see Marcy's underpants," the duo sang.

This did the trick; Marcy was up in a flash, ready to beat up her brother. Then she spied Royster in her brother's hair.

"I thought you liked the dollhouse," Marcy asked Royster. "Why did you move back into that booger head?"

Royster was shaking his head when Benji spoke up. "Marc, Grandma sold the dollhouse, and Harold and Ludwig are still inside."

"What?" Marcy yelled as she ran to shut her door.

Meanwhile, Harold and Ludwig were inside the closet, feeling as if they were in an earthquake. They could hear things falling all over the house. Then suddenly it stopped, and everything was quiet—however, not for long. They heard a car door open, and the movement started again. Then another loud slam and, *thud,* the house once again was still.

"Leeann," a voice yelled, "darlin', come see what Mommy bought you."

"What is this?" said a voice. "I asked for a pony, not a dumb old dollhouse."

Wow, thought Harold. He had never heard Marcy talk like this, so this must *not* be Marcy.

"Sweetie, sweetie, why don't you like it?" said the first voice.

This must be the mom, Ludwig thought.

"Look inside, baby. It's beautiful."

Ludwig leaned into Harold's ear. "What's wrong? Our house is beautiful."

"Shhhh," whispered Harold.

Just then, they heard the front door open, and with this, they scurried underneath the blankets stored in the closet.

"Look, the lights work." Then the closet door opened. "Look at the cute closet; there are even blankets." Then the hand took the corner of the yellow blanket, which was their hiding place.

"I don't want it, I don't. I don't," yelled the little girl.

The hand let go of the blanket and shut the front door, leaving the closet door ajar.

"Honey!" The mother's voice said. Then it faded, as she must have gotten farther away.

"Harold, let's run up to your room; there's more space to hide there," said Ludwig.

As he said this, he turned, only to see Harold's tail going up the stairs. Ludwig took off after him. The brothers climbed into Royster's closet because, after all, of the three of them, Royster was the "pack rat."

Things remained calm—at least for a while.

"Okay," said Marcy "who bought it?"

Benji never realized just how quickly his sister could get moving. Why couldn't she do that on school days?

"Marc, Marc, I don't know. I doubt if Royster knows. Do you?" he asked, looking at the frightened mouse.

"Nope!" Royster said, "Only that she had curlers in her hair and she was buying it for her little girl."

"Little girl …" puzzled Marcy.

"Did you hear any names?" added Benji.

"Mrs. P … I am pretty sure it started with a P," said the mouse, trying hard to help his brothers.

"I know," said Benji. "Marcy, you go into my room, into my closet, and then throw one of your famous "Marcy fits.""

"Hey!" said Marcy as Royster laughed under his breath. He didn't understand her shock, for he had seen plenty of these fits.

Marcy decided to take the high road and not argue; secretly she knew just what he meant.

"Well you go downstairs," said Marcy, "and get ready for my performance."

Marcy stood at the top of the stairs gathering her thoughts.

This has *to work*, she thought as she ran down the stairs.

"Mommy, Mommy, oh no, Mommy, where are you!" she yelled at the top of her voice.

Mrs. Hartford was folding towels in the laundry room when she heard Marcy's bloodcurdling scream. She immediately dropped the towels and ran into the living room.

"What? What?" she yelled.

Marcy grabbed her mother's leg. "Mommy, the dollhouse is gone. It's gone, Mom!"

Mrs. Hartford's heart skipped a beat, as she feared the worst for the three mouse brothers. She was about to start questioning Marcy when her mother walked into the room munching on a stalk of celery.

"Marcy, what in the world are you yelling about?" said Grandma. "Mary, darlin', you should really teach her to work on her inside voice."

"But, Mom!" said Marcy not looking at her grandma. "My dollhouse is G-O-N gone."

Mary Ellen interrupted, "You mean that dollhouse that was stuffed in the back of your brother's closet? Why, I sold it in the garage sale. It brought nearly ten dollars," said Grandma Parker, very proud of herself.

Mrs. Hartford's eyes flew open, and she coughed and sputtered.

"Mom, why did you sell that?" she finally managed to spit out. "That dollhouse was really special to our entire family."

Mrs. Parker rolled her eyes and walked toward the door.

"Darlin', that dollhouse was pushed way back in your son's closet; I doubt it has been played with in a while." And with that said, she walked outside.

Once she was outside and the door had shut behind her, Mrs. Hartford began to question Marcy.

"Did she ask you if she could sell it? Why did you let her …" Then she realized what she was saying. She knew that neither Marcy nor Benji would have let their grandma sell the dollhouse.

"Marcy, don't worry, sweetie; we will get it back. The mice will have their home. I promise," she said.

"But Mom the baddest thing is that Ludwig and Harold are still inside." Marcy was crying now, and these were *real* tears.

"*What!*" Mrs. Hartford yelled sitting down on the sofa before she fell onto the floor.

"Yep, Mom. Royster got out, but the other two are still in there," Marcy sat down beside her mother and began rubbing her arm.

"Benji, please come down here!" Mrs. Hartford yelled.

Benji came down the steps with Royster stuck in his shirt pocket. The mouse looked like he had seen a ghost, and truth be known, he had been through a lot that day.

"Royster, I am so sorry," Mrs. Hartford said as she took the small mouse into her hand. She began stroking his fur. "We are going to get your brothers back. I promise you that."

Mrs. Hartford went out into the garage to speak with her mom, knowing that if they were going to get the dollhouse back she would have to do it.

"Mom," she called out. "Mom, are you in here?"

"Mary, sweetie, I'm over here. I'm trying to get all of the garage sale things underneath the shelter. It looks like rain," Mrs. Parker said.

Mary walked over to her mother and said, "mom, who exactly bought the dollhouse?"

"It was Mrs. Pettigrew down the street. She said she was buying it for her daughter. She really fell in love with it once I showed her the lights and everything. Heck, you would have thought it came complete with an entire family," she finished.

Mrs. Hartford laughed nervously. "Now wouldn't that be funny?" she said to her mother.

"You see, Mom, Marcy's Grandma Hartford bought that for her, and the whole family pulled together to decorate it, so it's sort of special."

She looked into her mother's eyes to see if she was buying it. Mrs. Parker started into the house

"Marcy, Marcy, please come here to Grandma," she called out.

"What is it, Grandma? " Marcy asked wiping a fake tear from her eye.

"Darlin', Mrs. Pettigrew bought the dollhouse for Leeann. You know Leeann, don't you?" she asked.

Leeann Pettigrew, Marcy thought. *I should have known she had something to do with this.*

"Yes, ma'am," she said. "I know Leeann."

"Well, I will call Mrs. Pettigrew and explain it to her and see what we can do to get the dollhouse back," her grandma said.

Marcy sniffed and sniffed. "Okay, Grandma. I'm going to go to my room for awhile."

She slowly walked back inside; closing the door, she ran to her brother's room to explain.

Back at the Pettigrews, things were eerily quiet. Ludwig and Harold ventured out of their brother's closet to try to see if there was any way out of here. They slowly and carefully walked downstairs and into the living room.

"Let's look out the window and see if we can tell where we are," said Ludwig.

"Okay!" said Harold.

He slowly walked over to the window by the door and peered out. "Wh-what the …," he said to his brother. "Lud, come over here. You have gotta see this."

With that said, Ludwig came over and looked out, and he couldn't believe his eyes. On the table by the window in this strange house was a rat who looked not unlike themselves, but he was running on a wheel.

Chapter 4

Harold and Ludwig stared in amazement at the creature running on the wheel.

"Harold, are we seeing what I think we're seeing?" whispered Ludwig.

Harold said nothing; he simply stared in disbelief. They had always heard how their grandma had run around on a wheel at something called a college, but were they in college? He was confused.

"Ludwig," he said, "you stay here. I'm going to try to get over there and find out what's going on."

"No way, Harold, no way!" cried Ludwig "We're in this together. I'm going too."

"Okay," agreed Harold, "but stay with me; this could be very dangerous."

Mrs. Hartford dialed the phone quickly. She hoped that this would be easy. She had to get Harold and Ludwig back before any harm came to them. The phone rang once, twice.

"Hello," said a voice.

"Could I speak with Mrs. Pettigrew please?" said Mary Hartford.

"This is Mrs. Pettigrew," said the voice. "May I help you?"

"This is Mrs. Hartford," Mary began. "It seems that you just purchased a dollhouse from my garage sale."

"Yes, yes I did," said Mrs. Pettigrew. "I bought it for LeeAnn. LeeAnn is my darlin' little girl," she continued.

"Well—" Mrs. Hartford tried to interrupt, with no success.

"LeeAnn is such a brave little girl," she continued. "You see, LeeAnn had to go to the doctor yesterday, and she was so brave that ..."

"Yes, ma'am," Mrs. Hartford said. "Mrs. Pettigrew," she tried to continue.

"Please, call me Beatrice," said Mrs. Pettigrew.

"Well, Beatrice, it seems that my mother sold that dollhouse without asking Marcy, and she is quite upset about it," said Mrs. Hartford, attempting to sound desperate.

"Well, Mrs. Hartford, Mary, is it?"

"Yes," answered Mrs. Hartford.

"You see," continued Beatrice. "LeeAnn loves the dollhouse, and I don't know if she would be willing to part with it, but I would be glad to ask her."

"Oh please do, Beatrice. Please explain to her that Marcy's grandmother gave it to her and that my mother sold it by mistake," Mary pleaded.

"Mary, I will do my best," Mrs. Pettigrew said. "But I make no promises," she said as she hung up the phone.

Beatrice thought that she would wait until after dinner to mention the situation to her little angel.

Harold had stopped when he heard the telephone. The woman with curlers had answered it and had spoke at length about their house, or at least that is what he thought they were discussing.

Ludwig poked Harold on the shoulder and whispered, "Hey is she talkin' about our house?"

Harold nodded with his finger up over his lips, trying to get Ludwig to be quiet.

The minute the woman laid the phone down, Harold was ready to venture out to check out this place and see if he had any ideas on how they could get the heck out of here. Harold peeped out the door; the coast appeared to be clear. He grabbed Ludwig by the hand, and they ran under the sofa.

"Sweet-ums, I'm home!" said a voice in a singsong manner. "Bea, darlin' where are you?" It was a man's voice.

The woman, Bea, ran into the room.

Hey, where are the curlers? each mouse thought.

"Jimbo!" yelled the woman excitedly as she kissed him on the cheek. "I am so glad you're home. Did you have a good time?" she asked.

"This must be Mr. Pettigrew," whispered Harold to Ludwig, who still had his eyes shut from seeing the two adults kissing.

"What did she say, Mom?" asked Marcy as she wrung her hands.

"Well, she made no promises," said Mrs. Hartford, "but she says that she will ask LeeAnn."

"Hummph!" humphed Marcy. "That brat will never give up that dollhouse if she thinks I want it back."

"Mom, we *have* to get it back!" cried Benji loudly.

"We will," said Mom, trying to sound confident, "we will."

Mrs. Hartford went to the kitchen to start dinner; after all, Mr. Hartford would be back from the golf course shortly. Mrs. Hartford made chicken parmesan and a Caesar salad, and as she cooked, she could not help but think of the two missing mice; she wondered if they had enough to eat.

"Honey, I'm home!" came a voice from the living room.

Ben, Mary thought, *I have to explain this to him before …*

"Daddy, Daddy!" screamed Marcy and Benji in unison as they ran into the room.

"What is it, kids?" said their dad. "Slow down; slow down."

"Daddy!" both kids said at once.

"Calm down; one at a time, please," said Mr. Hartford.

"Daddy," said Benji. "Grandma Parker sold the dollhouse, and"—Royster stuck his head out of Benji's shirt pocket—"his brothers are inside."

"What?" Mr. Hartford cried in disbelief. "Mary!" he yelled.

"What is all the racket?" said Mrs. Parker coming downstairs. "I see Marcy isn't the only loud person in this family. Ben, really must you yell?"

Exasperated, Mr. Hartford went looking for his wife. Finding her in the kitchen, he said, "Mary, can I please see you in the garage?"

Ben followed Mary into the garage. "Mary, what has gone on here today?" he asked.

"Well, Mom sold the dollhouse to Beatrice Pettigrew for little LeeAnn," said Mary.

Mr. Hartford stood with his mouth opened wide.

Royster had ducked down inside Benji's pocket just as soon as he'd heard *her* voice. Oh, how he wished he could run up to her and scare the bejeezus out of her; after all, she deserved it if anyone did. He could not stop thinking of Harold and Ludwig; he sure hoped that they would be okay until they could get them back home. They would get them home … wouldn't they?

"Honey!" said the man, who must be Mr. Pettigrew, father to little LeeAnn "Brattygrew," as Marcy often called her.

"I have a surprise for LeeAnn. Is she in her room?"

"Yes," said Mrs. Pettigrew. "LeeAnn!" she shrieked. "Come here, honey. Daddy's home."

"So what!" yelled LeeAnn from her room. "Tell him to come here. I'm in my room, and my shot arm hurts."

"What?" questioned her dad.

"Oh, she had a vaccination yesterday—poor baby; let's go to her room."

Mrs. P hopped off the couch and grabbed Mr. Pettigrew by the arm. She was twice his size and four times as loud.

"Wait, let me go get the surprise," he said walking out the door.

Ludwig craned his neck; oh how he loved surprises. The front door opened, and Harold nearly fainted at what he saw.

"Marcy, help Mama clear these dishes," said Mrs. Hartford. She said this because she needed to talk with Marcy alone.

"I'll help you, Mary," said Mrs. Parker stacking the dishes.

"Oh no, Mom," interjected Mary. "Marcy needs to help with chores." With this, she winked at Marcy.

"Yep, Mom," said Marcy. "I'm ready to be your slave."

"Oh, okay, Marcy," said her mother, rolling her eyes.

Once they were in the kitchen, Marcy was instructed to call LeeAnn and plead for her dollhouse.

"Plead!" yelled Marcy. "With that B-R … B-R, well however you spell it—brat. No way, Mom!"

"Marcy, Harold and Lud are counting on us," said Mrs. Hartford.

"Okay, for the meese," said Marcy.

"Mice," her mom corrected.

Royster and Benji went out on the porch. The air was crisp, and there was a slight breeze. Fall was here, and soon winter would be here, bringing cold and snow. Benji had looked forward to taking the mice out and letting them help him with his snow fort. Why, his mom had even offered to make them snow suits. He had to get Harold and Ludwig back; he just had to.

Chapter 5

Ring. Ring. The Pettigrew's phone began to ring. Harold and Ludwig ducked back under the sofa to make sure no one saw them.

"Coming, coming!" yelled Mrs. Pettigrew.

In the meantime, Mr. P came into view and Mrs. P shrieked.

"Hello," she said mouth standing wide open. She was surprised by what her husband was holding in his hands.

"Hello," she repeated.

"LeeAnn is busy right now. Can I get her to call you back?" she continued.

"Marcy," she repeated. "Okay, she will call you after dinner."

She hung up the phone and kissed her husband dead on the lips. "Jim, darlin', she is going to *love* this."

They climbed the stairs together to surprise their only child.

"Ludwig, did I see what I thought I saw?" Harold asked.

GULP, gulped Ludwig. "Y-Y-Yes it, it w-w-was a kkkkkkitten, Harold," Ludwig managed to stutter.

"What are we gonna do, Harold?" cried Ludwig.

"We got trouble now, huh, Harold," Ludwig added.

Ludwig was scared, as was Harold; they knew this little bundle of fur could spell trouble for two little lost mice.

"LeeAnn, sweetie, look what Daddy brought you," said Mrs. Pettigrew as she and her husband entered LeeAnn's room.

"Ooohh, Daddy!" yelled LeeAnn. "Daddy, Daddy, thank you, Daddy."

LeeAnn loved this little black kitten. She wanted a kitten more than she wanted a pony. She could scarcely contain her joy.

"I'm gonna name him Larry," she told her daddy as she kissed him over and over again.

"Well, honey," said her dad, "there is only one problem with that; he is a she, so you may want to change that name."

"Okay, okay. I think I'll call her Samantha, Sammie for short," she decided.

"Sammie, it is," said Mrs. Pettigrew.

"This is a great present, Daddy," said Marcy in her best daddy's girl voice, "better than some ol' dollhouse."

"Baby, about that dollhouse," Mrs. Pettigrew began, "Marcy's mom called today about maybe getting it back. It seems that her grandma sold it when they didn't really want to part with it."

LeeAnn's eyes lit up. *Hmmmm!* she thought. "Well, Mama, I do kinda like it, ya know," she said.

She was thinking that this may be the perfect opportunity to get little Miss Marcy just where she wanted her. Sammie purred in her ear. Tonight she would enjoy her new kitten; tomorrow she would worry about the dollhouse.

"Mommy, Mommy!" Marcy said, trying hard not to cry. "I called LeeAnn, but she was busy. Now, Mom, how busy can that brat be?"

"Now, Marcia Jane Hartford!" Mrs. Hartford said sternly. "LeeAnn knew nothing about the mice or the dollhouse. Her mother bought it, remember?"

"I know, I know, Mommy but—" Marcy burst into tears, grabbing her mom by the neck.

Mr. and Mrs. Pettigrew went into the kitchen to catch up. Harold and Ludwig watched their feet go by the sofa.

Once they had passed, Ludwig whispered to Harold, "Let's go, bro. We gotta make it to the rat over there."

Harold and Ludwig tiptoed over to the chair and climbed up; if they stretched as far as they could, they just might make it. Just then, the wheel stopped turning, and the rat-like creature looked up at the two adventurous brothers.

"Hey, just who do you think you are?" he said.

"H-Harold, I think he's talkin' to us," stuttered Ludwig.

"Hi, I'm Harold, and this here is my brother, Ludwig," said Harold as he pulled himself onto the table in front of the metal thing that held this creature.

"Hey, Harold and Lud-Ludwig, is it?" said the rat. "My name is Jack, but the girl here calls me Flash," he continued.

"Well hello, Jack," said Ludwig. "How did you get in there?" he added.

"I am what is called a hamster, and I came from a pet store. They put me in this cage, and I get fed and get to run around on this wheel all day," said Jack.

"Looks like fun," said Harold.

"Sometimes she takes me out, and I get to run around in this round thing—out there on the floor. Now *that* is fun," said Jack.

Just then, they heard LeeAnn bounding down the steps.

"Mommy, Sammie's hungry."

Ludwig and Harold ducked behind the thing Jack had called a cage.

"I know, Roy; let's go for a bike ride," said Benji to the mouse peeking out of his pocket.

"Okay, Ben, maybe that will help take my mind off things," sighed Royster.

They took off down the street toward the Pettigrew house. Benji thought he might just stop and plead with them on his sister's behalf. As they neared 126 Sharpe Street, Benjamin could scarcely believe his eyes, for sitting in the window next to a hamster cage were Harold and Ludwig.

"Roy!" shouted Benji. "Look, it's your brother's there in the window."

Royster looked up; his heart nearly jumped out of his chest. "Ben, we gotta go get 'em," yelled the mouse, "we gotta!"

"Hold on, hold on," said Benjamin. "Let me think."

He didn't see anyone else in the living room, so he crept up to the window. The mice had their little behinds pressed up to the window, apparently hiding from something. Benji knelt behind the shrubs, and tapped on the window.

Harold jumped, afraid to move. Ludwig turned to see Roy and Benji staring back at him.

"Harold, Harold," he whispered.

"Shhhh, Lud!" Harold said. "Ya wanna get caught? Now SHHHH!"

Ludwig waved furiously at the familiar faces. It was then that Benji saw the Pettigrews coming in from the kitchen. Benji fell into the azaleas, nearly dropping Royster.

"Jim, it was so sweet of you to buy that kitten for LeeAnn," Mrs. Pettigrew gushed. "She is so good with animals. She has always taken such care of Flash."

"Bea," Mr. Pettigrew asked, "I heard you talking to LeeAnn about the dollhouse."

"Yes," she started to explain, "I bought it from the Hartford's garage sale, but it seems that Mary's mother sold it without asking the family."

Beatrice and Jim were busy discussing this when LeeAnn skipped into the room carrying Sammie. She had put one of her hair ribbons into Sammie's tail, which seemed to upset the kitten terribly.

"Mama," she asked, "can I let Flash run in his ball so Sammie can get to know him?"

"Well, honey," her mom explained, "rats and kittens aren't usually the best of friends."

"But, Mommy!" LeeAnn cried. "Flash is a"hampster"not a rat."

Mrs. Pettigrew laughed. "Well I suppose, in that case." She took the ball from the closet and went to retrieve the "hampster."

Benji got up onto his knees and checked to make sure Royster was still there.

"Roy," he whispered, "you still there, buddy?"

"Yeah, man, I'm okay," said Royster.

Benji leaned up a little farther and peered into the living room window. The mice were still behind the cage, and Mrs. P was coming toward it with one of those exercise balls. She would surely spy the intruders if she removed the hamster. Benji thought quickly and crawled to the front door. He rang the doorbell quickly.

Ding-dong! the bell sounded in the Pettigrew home.

"Coming," called Mrs. P.

The door opened just as Benji decided what he had to do.

"Mrs. Pettigrew, is LeeAnn home?" he asked politely.

"Sure. And you are Benjamin Hartford; am I right?"

"Yes, ma'am," said Benji.

"Come inside Benji," called Mr. Pettigrew from the living room.

Royster was now cowering inside Benji's pocket, praying he wouldn't be noticed.

"LeeAnn," said her mother, "Benjamin Hartford is here to see you."

LeeAnn came into the hallway carrying Sammie, who was surfing the air questioningly.

"Look, Benji, what my daddy brought back from his trip," LeeAnn said holding Sammie close to Benji.

"Meow," said Sammie, reaching for Benji's pocket with one of her paws.

Oh no! thought Benji. *Roy!*

"Aaa Choooo!" he sneezed. "I'm allergic," said Benji.

"Bless you," said Mr. Pettigrew.

"LeeAnn," Benji started, "have you thought about selling the dollhouse back to Marcy? She misses it something fierce."

"Well," said LeeAnn, "I love it so much." As she said this her parents glared at her. "But," she added, "for $19.99 I might could part with it."

"Nineteen ninety-nine!" yelled Benji. "Didn't your mom only pay $9.99 for it?"

"LeeAnn Beatrice Pettigrew!" yelled her mom.

"Well, Mommy." LeeAnn started to cry and ran to her room, kitten and all.

"Benjamin," explained LeeAnn's dad. "I am sorry for that, but it may take awhile to talk some sense into her. What if I call you when she is ready to sell?"

"Yes, sir," said Benji trying to hide his extreme anger and disappointment.

"Please call soon," he added as he walked out the door.

Benji and Royster walked out of that house feeling defeated. Royster knew his brothers needed him more than ever now. He was their only hope. As they walked up the street, they glanced back into the window. Harold and Ludwig had managed to run and hide, for that much Royster was grateful.

Marcy went to bed early that night; she needed to rest if she were going to get the mice back. She needed to come up with some sort of plan. She might consider LeeAnn to be the world's biggest brat, but she was going to give her a run for her money.

Back at the Pettigrew house things settled down for the night. Sammie and LeeAnn had snuggled together after her daddy had read them a bedtime story. Actually, Harold and Ludwig were hiding in LeeAnn's pajama drawer, so they had also enjoyed the story. Harold finally knew that those three bears had caught Goldilocks. He had always fallen asleep when Benji told them that story. Now it made a little more sense to him. Once Mr. Pettigrew had finished his story, he tucked LeeAnn into bed, kissing her he turned out the light.

"Good night, sweetie," he said as he shut the door, leaving it open a crack.

"Ludwig, Ludwig!" Harold whispered. "Lud," he said turning around.

Ludwig had snuggled down into LeeAnn's purple, flannel pj's, and he was about to start snoring. Harold tapped his brother on the shoulder.

Ludwig awoke with a start. "Someone's been sleeping in *my* bed," he said sleepily.

"Ludwig, wake up. We gotta get out of here," said Harold.

The two stood up and peered out of the crack in the drawer. They climbed down quietly. LeeAnn snored, and unless their ears were playing tricks on them, so did Sammie. They dropped off the drawer onto the pillow below; whew, it was a long was down, at least to a little mouse. Once onto the floor, Harold looked around to see what their next move would be.

"Purrrrr," he heard the kitten purring; at least that meant she was asleep. Just then, they heard movement on the bed above.

"Ludwig!" Harold called out.

"Yeah, Harold," answered Ludwig.

"When I say three, we are going to run into the hallway and go underneath the little table out there." Harold gave Ludwig details of his plan.

"One, two," he began, but just as he was about to say *three*, Ludwig took off around him and into the hallway.

Harold ran after him. Once underneath the table, Harold started lecturing Ludwig on the importance of staying together. Ludwig was only half listening because his heart was still beating with anticipation of what would come next.

"Where to now?" asked Ludwig.

"Well," said Harold, "I think that just down this hallway we will find the stairs, and then we take the stairs to the living room. I think so anyways," finished Harold.

Ludwig peered out; the coast was clear, so they made a run for it. Down the hall they went. Once on the stairs, they took them one at a time, carefully. There were only six of them, but there may as well have been a million; after all, Harold and Ludwig were tiny, little mice.

"Whew!" Ludwig sighed when they reached the bottom. "We made it, huh, Harold?" said Ludwig, leaning against the wall to catch his breath.

Looking up the stairs the two mice saw a sliver of light appear. The footsteps came closer and closer to the stairs; it was Mr. Pettigrew. He yawned really big, scratching his head and making his sparse head of hair stand on ends. Ludwig tried hard not to laugh at this hilarious sight. Harold grabbed Ludwig's little hand and dragged him out of the way. Mr. P. walked down the stairs and into the kitchen. Opening the refrigerator, he pulled out the salami and cheese and the gallon of milk.

Sniff, sniff.

Harold sniffed the air. *Cheese*, he thought. He *knew* he smelled cheese, and everyone knew what cheese did to him.

"Provolone," whispered Harold.

"Fight it, bro!" said Ludwig, holding onto his brother by the nape of the neck.

"Ch-ch-cheese!" said Harold. Cheeseeeeeeeeee."

"Harold," said Ludwig, slapping his brother across the face, "Snap out of it, bro, do you want to get caught?"

Harold, after being slapped, shook his head.

"Oh my God, Lud, what did I do?" asked Harold.

"Nothing, brother, but that was a close call," said Ludwig.

Marcy slept fitfully that night. She tossed and turned, and she dreamed. She dreamt she was in the Pettigrew house looking for her dollhouse and the two mice brothers. She entered a room; it was all pink with ruffles everywhere.

"What are you doing in my room?" yelled a voice.

Turning, she noticed it was Princess Bratzilla, LeeAnn herself. She was sitting in the middle of her bed eating little squares of cheese.

"What are you looking for, Marcy?" asked LeeAnn.

"LeeAnn, I am tired of begging. I want my dollhouse, and I want it now," yelled Marcy.

"Okay, you can have your dumb ol' dollhouse," LeeAnn said, picking up something off the bed.

"Wh-what do you mean, I can have it?" Marcy said.

"I mean you can have the dollhouse, but you cannot have these," she said, holding up what appeared to be something that looked alive. "Why, I love these little things more than I love my collection of Pretty Pet Ponies."

Marcy looked over in the direction LeeAnn was pointing and noticed probably nine or ten ponies with long, colorful manes that you could actually comb.

Oh my God, it cannot be, she thought to herself, realizing what the things she was holding were.

"Have what?" asked Marcy, pretending not to know what she was talking about.

"These," said LeeAnn, holding Harold and Ludwig up in her hand; each mouse was eating a square of cheese.

"Hi, Marcy!" said Harold with a mouthful of mozzarella. "What are you doing here?"

"Marcy, Marcy, Marcy," yelled Ludwig, holding a square in each hand, "we love our new home."

"Ludwig, Harold!" Marcy yelled. "I'm so glad to see that you're okay. Are you ready to go home to see Royster? He's been crazy with worry."

"Royster, Schmoyster, we ain't missin' no Royster!" said Harold with yet another mouthful of cheese.

"Yeah," said Harold, "we love it here, and we are stayin'!'"

"No, no!" yelled Marcy aloud as she began to toss and turn in her bed. "Come with me. We love you, and Benji hasn't been the same without you."

Marcy's mom walked into the room, only to see her little girl tossing and turning in the bed.

"Marcy, Marcy," Mrs. Hartford said. "Sweetheart, wake up. Marcy, wake up."

Suddenly Marcy sat straight up in the bed

"Mom, we gotta get Lud and Harold back, *now*!" she yelled.

She went on and on about her dream. Her mother listened intently and then went about reassuring her that the mice would never like another family as much as they loved the Hartfords.

Marcy finally calmed down and said to her mom, "Well, Mom, I'm still going to try to get them back. I gotta get them back."

"Okay, sweetie, but right now, get downstairs for breakfast because Grandma wants to get on the road," said her mother.

"Okay, Mom, I'll be there shortly," said Marcy, getting out of the bed.

Morning came quickly for Harold and Ludwig. Last night had been a scary experience. The two mice had almost been caught, and they knew they had to be more careful. Today they decided that they would make it back to the dollhouse and hope that the Hartford's would rescue them soon. They had slept underneath the kitchen table that night, hoping they would wake up before the rest of the family. Upon waking, they headed for the living room to find the dollhouse. The last time they'd seen it, it was beside the front door. Harold stuck his head out from under the table and saw nothing, so they went toward the living room.

"Mom, Mom," said Marcy as she ran down the stairs and straight into her grandmother.

"Marcy, give Grandma a hug," said her grandmother with her arms outstretched, "a big ol' hug." Mrs. Parker kissed her granddaughter on the head.

"Oh morning, Gran," said Marcy

"Mom, Mom," she added.

"Marcy, what are you screaming about?" said her mother as she came around the corner and into the dining room with a plate of pancakes.

"Mom, can I talk to you in the kitchen?" asked Marcy as she motioned her head toward the kitchen.

"Marcy, Grandma is going to leave in an hour, and we need to eat breakfast," said her mom sighing but walking toward the kitchen. "Mom, go ahead and start eating; we will be back shortly," said Mary.

"Okay, but don't be long; the pancakes won't stay warm forever," said Mrs. Parker, sitting down to eat.

Once in the kitchen Marcy started rattling off what was on her mind.

"Mom, you know my dream," she said. "you know I was at LeAnn's, she had the mice, and she wouldn't—"

"Stop. Take a breath, Marcy, take a breath!" said Mrs. Hartford.

"Mom, she wouldn't give up Harold and Lud, but I think I got an idea from that dream, Mom," Marcy added quickly.

"Okay, let's hear it," said her mother.

"Well, Mom, I forgot how much LeeAnn loves the Pet Ponies."

"Pet ponies?" asked Mrs. Hartford.

"Yeah they're toys, Mom, and she just *might* give us the dollhouse if we trade." Marcy finished her sentence, and suddenly she felt sure she would get her dollhouse back now.

"Marcy, don't get your hopes up, honey," said Mrs. Parker walking into the kitchen.

Marcy and her mom looked at one another

"Mom, how long have you been standing there?" asked Mary.

"Marcy, she may give you your dollhouse and maybe not. Please don't get too excited."

"Well, Grandma, I have ten dollars, and I'm going to the store and buy a couple of ponies," said Marcy. "And then I'm going to offer LeeAnn a trade."

Benji rolled over to see Royster staring out the window. "What are you doing buddy?" asked Benji of his little mouse friend.

"I am just wishing that I had stayed in that dollhouse," he said, never turning around. "At least we would be together."

Benji realized that Royster was crying.

"Roy, please don't cry," said Benji climbing out of bed. "I'm going downstairs. Grandma is leaving today …"

"Hummph …" said Royster.

"Roy, please don't do this," pleaded Benji. "I promise Grandma didn't mean to do it. Why, she didn't even know what she was doing."

"I know, Ben, I know. But those two are the only family I have," sniffed Royster. "Imagine if someone stole Marcy."

"Hmmmmmm," sighed Benji. "Yeah, that would be awful," he said.

Benji went downstairs to eat breakfast as Royster stared out the window.

"How are you two doing?" he said quietly, staring out the window in the direction of the Pettigrew's. "Hang in there. I'm going to see to it that you make it home."

The two mice brothers had made their way back to the dollhouse by morning. Daybreak found both of them sleeping underneath a pile of blankets in the living room closet.

"Lud, Lud," Harold whispered as he poked his brother in the side, "wake up, Ludwig."

"Okay, okay, I'm up, Harold. Stop poking me."

Ludwig dug himself from under the blankets, stretching as he came up.

"Harold, what's for breakfast?" asked Ludwig.

"Lud, we have to stay here and hope and pray Ben and Royster save us in time," Harold explained.

"In time for wh-wh-what?" asked Ludwig.

"Don't think about that, Ludwig," said Harold. "They will come for us."

The family finished their breakfast, and Grandma Parker went in to pack her things.

"Marcy!" Grandma called from upstairs.

Marcy went up to see her. "Yes, ma'am," she said.

"Marcy, I am so sorry for selling your dollhouse," she began. "If I had known how important it was to you, I would have never sold it."

"Grandma, I know," said Marcy hugging her grandma. "I'm going to get it back."

"Well, Marcy, if I had an extra day I would go with you to offer the ponies because I think that is going to work," said Grandma Parker.

"I sure hope so," said Marcy, turning to go back into the kitchen.

Mrs. Parker decided that she had to make one stop before she left town.

"Sweetie," shrieked Mrs. Pettigrew, "breakfast is ready. LeeAnn are you up, baby?"

Ludwig and Harold cringed and pulled the blankets tighter over their heads.

"Coming, honey!" called Mr. Pettigrew as he came down the stairs.

LeeAnn bounded down the steps almost knocking her daddy off his feet.

"Hungry, Lee baby?" her dad asked.

"No, no, Daddy. Sammie isn't in my room, and I'm looking for her," she said.

"Meow."

The mice heard the sound, they had been dreading.

The kitten sniffed and sniffed. She knew there was something in there, and she was determined to get to it. Sammie's paw managed to open the front door of the dollhouse; then she managed to get her cold little nose through the doorway.

"Meow," she said, which meant, "I know you're in here somewhere."

Suddenly, the closet door, the only thing between the mice and sure *trouble*, began to shake.

"Ludwig," whispered Harold. "Do you think the C-A-T can get in?"

"No, no," whispered Ludwig back to his brother, "we're safe in here." He was trying to convince himself of this fact.

Scratch, scratch—the noise continued.

"Sammie, there you are," shouted LeeAnn. "What's in that old dollhouse?"

LeeAnn picked up the kitten and headed toward the kitchen.

"Mommy, we're coming, and Sammie is hungry," shouted LeeAnn.

Once out of earshot, Harold pulled himself out from under the blankets and peered out of the closet door. Then he bravely crept into the living room and looked out of the door.

"Whew!" he sighed. For now, they were safe, but he did not know how long that would last.

The Pettigrews ate breakfast together while Sammie dined next to LeeAnn—yes, on the table right next to her.

Suddenly, there was the sound of the doorbell.

"Now who could that be so early?" said Jim as he went to open the door.

"Coming, coming," he called out as he reached for the door.

Opening the door, he found an older woman standing before him.

"May I help you?" he said.

"Come in, Mrs. Parker," said Beatrice, who was now standing behind him. "What can we do for you, Mary Ellen?" she continued.

"Is LeeAnn here?" asked Mary Ellen, looking toward the kitchen.

"What, Mommy?" called LeeAnn from the kitchen.

"Come in here, sweetie. Marcy's grandmother would like to see you," said Mrs. Pettigrew.

LeeAnn rolled her eyes. She knew this had to have something to do with that dumb old dollhouse.

"Yes, Mom," said LeeAnn. "Hi, Mrs., Mrs., Marcy's grandma."

"It's Mrs. Parker," laughed Mrs. Pettigrew.

"Mrs. Parker," said LeeAnn.

"Mr. and Mrs. Pettigrew, can I please speak with LeeAnn alone?" asked Mary Ellen.

"Sure," said Mr. Pettigrew, looking at this wife for her approval.

"Sure," said Beatrice, standing up to go into the kitchen; after all, her omelet was getting cold.

Chapter 6

"Mommy," asked Marcy, "can we go to the toy store when it opens?"

"Sure, honey," said her mom, hoping her daughter had not gotten her hopes up too high.

Mrs. Hartford washed the breakfast dishes while Marcy got herself dressed. While she washed, she found her mind focused on the two missing mice brothers. She never would have thought she'd become so attached to a rodent. She missed their mischievous nature. Why, she even missed cleaning up their cheesy messes.

Mrs. Parker talked to LeeAnn for about twenty minutes. She explained Marcy's plan; she explained how she hoped that LeeAnn could somehow accept Marcy's offer. She spoke with her about the importance of the dollhouse, not only to Marcy, but also to the entire Hartford family. She was finished. She had said all she could say; now the ball was in LeeAnn's court.

"Have a nice trip home, Mrs. ... Mrs. Marcy's grandma," said LeeAnn as she pondered what she should do.

Mrs. Hartford and Marcy drove to the toy store. Marcy was quiet the entire way; that was quite unusual. They pulled up to Stevenson's, and Mrs. Hartford got out of the car. She looked back at Marcy, who had her eyes closed.

"Marcy, honey," Mary said quietly, "we're here."

"I know, Mom. I was praying," she said with a tear in her eye. "We gotta get 'em back; we got to."

"Come on, dear," said Mrs. Hartford, shutting the car door.

Once inside the store, Marcy ran toward the Pet Pony aisle. The store must have had twenty different ponies. They had yellow ones, purple ones, pink ones, rainbow, ones—you name it; they had it. Marcy was deciding which two she wanted when she heard a voice.

"Hi, little lady; you are lucky. It's almost Christmas, and you're getting a new toy."

Looking up, Marcy saw an older woman.

"No, ma'am, I'm giving these away," Marcy explained. "Well I'm trying to help my brother and his best friends."

"You're one special little girl," said the woman as she walked away.

Marcy looked up at her mom, who smiled as she wiped a tear. Her little girl now knew the importance of doing something to help someone else. She was thinking of someone else instead of herself. Mrs. Hartford had never been prouder.

Royster could barely eat the cheese pancakes Mrs. Hartford had made for him. He was sick with worry over his brothers. He imagined that they were hungry, but most of all he imagined that they were scared. He was starting to lose hope that he would see them again.

There was a knock on the Pettigrew's door.

"Who now?" said Mr. Pettigrew, coming from his study.

He opened the door and saw a little girl he recognized as a classmate of LeeAnn's. "LeeAnn, someone's here to see you," he called up the stairs.

LeeAnn came down the stairs one at a time. She dreaded the meeting; she looked around the corner knowing what she must do.

"Marcy, hey, what are you doing here?" said LeeAnn.

"LeeAnn , you know I want my dollhouse back real bad," said Marcy, trying not to cry. "So I decided that I would buy you these two ponies so maybe you would trade with me."

LeeAnn just looked at her, not saying a word.

"My mom sent the money to your mom, the money she paid for it," said Marcy, handing LeeAnn the money.

LeeAnn took the money and peered into the Stevenson's Toy Store bag.

"I bought the rainbow and the yellow ponies. I hope you like them,"
said Marcy, taking them from the bag.

Mrs. Hartford sat in the car, keeping her fingers crossed, still not believing how proud she was of her little girl. She picked up her cell phone to call Benjamin; maybe if he said a little prayer it might help; it couldn't hurt.

"Benji," said Mrs. Hartford into the phone, "tell Royster to hold on. Hopefully we will have his brothers home before lunch."

"What?" The mouse had heard the message, "My brothers home." Royster crossed his fingers and his little rodent toes; why, he even bent his tail into a pretzel shape. Whatever Marcy and Mrs. Hartford were doing, it just *had* to work.

Mrs. Hartford saw Marcy step out of the Pettigrew house; she tried to read her expression. Oh no—she was still holding the plastic bag from the toy store. Wait, there was someone else coming out of the house. It was Beatrice, followed by LeeAnn. Bea spoke to LeeAnn as they followed Marcy. Mrs. Pettigrew smiled as she talked.

"Mary," said Mrs. Pettigrew, still smiling. "LeeAnn has something to tell you."

"Mrs. Hartford," said LeeAnn, "I 'cided that I'm givin' the dollhouse back."

Mary tried not to yell, but she was so excited.

"I was happy that Marcy was going to give me the ponies, but I have ten of them," Leeann said, smiling at Marcy.

"And," said Mrs. Pettigrew, nudging her daughter.

"Oh yeah," said LeeAnn, "I just want her to have the dollhouse, and I want her to keep the ponies. She will love them as much as me."

LeeAnn finished and smiled up at her mom. Mrs. Pettigrew beamed with pride. She had never been prouder of her daughter. Mrs. Hartford stared at Mrs. Pettigrew; she understood exactly how she felt. Marcy could not believe her eyes.

Mr. Pettigrew was coming down the sidewalk toward their car. Mrs. Hartford's heart skipped a beat when she saw he was carrying the dollhouse. Mary opened her door. "Let me help you with that." She opened the back door, and Mr. Pettigrew gently placed the precious cargo inside. Mrs. Hartford glanced inside the dollhouse windows to see if there was any sign of the mice brothers; no such luck.

Shutting the back door, she walked over to LeeAnn. She placed one hand on the girl's shoulder, and leaning down, she whispered, "LeeAnn, we are so grateful for what you have done. You will be blessed for this."

LeeAnn blushed. "It's okay; I know how important this is to Marcy."

LeeAnn turned to go into the house thinking, *Hey, this niceness feels pretty good.*

Chapter 7

"Roy, what is wrong, buddy?"

Royster looked up, careful to keep everything crossed.

"Your mom called. She may be bringing my brothers home—*home!*"Benji heard his mom's car pull into the garage. He picked up Royster, placing him in his pocket. "Let's go, buddy, but don't get your hopes up."

"Okay, okay, let's just go," yelled Royster.

Mary and Marcy were smiling ear to ear.

"Mom, do you have 'em?" yelled Benji.

"Well?" screamed Royster.

"We have the house, but I haven't seen inside," said Marcy.

Mrs. Hartford removed the dollhouse very carefully from the car. Benji opened the door for his mom, peering inside as she walked by.

The movement stopped and so had the noise. Harold and Ludwig knew that noise; it was a car. There was no telling what had happened this time. Hold on a minute—could it be? It sure sounded like Royster.

"Hey, Lud, did you hear what I heard?" whispered Harold.

"Huh," said Ludwig, still buried deep underneath the covers.

"Lud, I think I heard Royster," said Harold, opening the closet door a crack.

Suddenly the house started to move again. Harold shut the door and joined his brother."Okay, Benji, put Royster down and let him check it out," said Marcy.

Benji gingerly placed Roy on the floor. "Okay, Roy, go inside. Go on, go on."

Royster opened the front door peering inside. "Ahem," he cleared his throat. "Harold, Ludwig," he repeated over and over, softly at first getting louder each time.

Harold's ears perked up. "It's Royster," Harold shouted, digging out from underneath the covers. Ludwig pulled himself out, tripping over his own feet. The two brothers grabbed the closet doorknob at the same time.

"Royster" they shouted in unison as the door opened.

"Harold, Ludwig," shouted Royster, fighting back the tears.

They grabbed one another and hugged and hugged none of them wanting to let go. Mrs. Hartford, Benji, and Marcy stared in the windows of the dollhouse watching this joyous reunion. Benji put his arm around Marcy, who reached up and patted his hand.

"Marcy, thanks, sis. Without you, the boys would still be at the Pettigrews," said Benji.

"Aww, it's okay," said Marcy. "I didn't do nuttin'."

Mrs. Hartford grinned. She had witnessed her younger, usually selfish daughter become caring and totally selfless, and for that, she was thankful.

The mice once again became comfortable in their dollhouse home. Mr. and Mrs. Hartford made a place for the dollhouse in the living room so the mice could enjoy the family movie nights as well as family game night. Mr. Hartford had even built a stable for the ponies to live in. The brothers called them Isabella and Roxanne. They couldn't ride them, but it was fun to comb their manes and have their pictures taken while sitting up in the saddle.

October soon turned to November, which meant Thanksgiving was just around the corner. Thanksgiving meant another visit from Grandma Parker. The mice lived in fear of what havoc she might wreak this time.

Printed in the United States
By Bookmasters